CW01287980

Programme Management – Delivery Manual
Leadership and Governance, Demand Management

About the Author
Dodo Lilly-West is a highly experienced business and IT professional with almost two decades track record of accomplishments within, blue-chip FTSE 100 companies and the public sector. An expert in programme management, business development and building / leading high performing local, regional and global teams. He has been a Program Director, Program Manager, Project Manager and held various hands on management consulting positions in several companies. Dodo has several industry memberships and certifications including: Project Management Institute (PMI), ITIL Service Management, Association for Project Management (APM), Managing Successful Programmes (MSP) and Prince2. He also holds a Business Studies degree and a Masters in International Finance and Political Relations. Dodo is available for speaking and providing training opportunities. Please contact him at dodo.lilly.west@gmail.com.

About This Book
This book provides you with the Leadership & Governance and Demand Management information you need to plan, setup, run and deliver a programme comprising of any number of projects. It is exhaustive, in depth and treats the underpinning factors and features of what is required to deliver a programme successfully. Depending on the size of the engagement or initiative, programme managers or senior management will find that they can use the steps described in this book to develop and tailor their programme structure to the appropriate size.

Each discipline comprises of the main functions and each function drills down providing details of what is required to plan, setup, run and deliver that function. Each function details the required expertise necessary to carry out and implement the responsibilities. The fundamental inputs and output deliverables necessary to progress each discipline and function are provided. Inputs from prior stages feed into the next and future stages in the programme plan and life cycle.

Within each functional area you will find vital steps and recommendations. By following the vital steps a program Manager or Senior Manager will be able to fulfil best practice activities and steps that result in the desired outcome.

Assumptions

In the interest of time and space I have made several assumptions about you the reader:

> You have mastered the basic principles of project management
>
> You appreciate that although there are areas of similarities and touch points, programme management is not the same discipline as a project management.
>
> You understand that programme management encompasses project management and deals with delivery from a broader and more exhaustive vantage point.
>
> You appreciate that the Leadership and Governance and Demand Management duties in programme management deals with a broader spectrum of management

Additional Support

Please visit www.vitdesot.com for templates and deliverable samples.

Published by VITDESoT 2015
34 New House, 67-68 Hatton Garden, London, EC1N 8JY

ISBN-13: 978-1508805038

Copyright ©2015 by VITDESoT Ltd United Kingdom.

Part Series Also By Dodo Lilly-West

Programme Management – Delivery Manual: Programme Delivery, Programme Control and Administration, Resource Management, Delivery Management

Programme Management – Delivery Manual: Stakeholder Acceptance, Stakeholder Management

Programme Management – Delivery Manual: Value Management, Value Measurement, Quality Management

Table of Contents

1. Leadership and Governance
   - Leadership and Governance　　　　　　　　1 - 7
   - Assess Current Leadership Capabilities　　8 - 9
   - Define Governance Approach　　　　　　　10 - 12
   - Develop Leadership Initiatives　　　　　　　13 - 15
   - Implement the Governance Organization　　16 - 18
   - Implement Leadership Initiatives　　　　　　19 - 20
   - Sustain Leadership Commitment　　　　　　21 - 22

2. Demand Management
   - Develop Program and Project Inventory　　23 - 25
   - Prioritize Project List　　　　　　　　　　　26
   - Plan Capacity and Utilization　　　　　　　　27
   - Align Budget　　　　　　　　　　　　　　　28
   - Finalize Project List　　　　　　　　　　　　29

Chapter 1

Leadership and Governance

Understand Goals and Expectations

Aims and Objectives

Understand Goals and Expectations is the primary process to document stakeholder expectations, assign responsibility for key stakeholders, determine performance measures, and define the monitoring approach.

The Manage Stakeholder Expectations and Satisfaction task documents the steps for continuing the confirmation of these goals and expectations, collection and analysis of stakeholder satisfaction, and continuous alignment of changed goals and expectations. The Stakeholder Management activity refines, verifies, implements, and monitors measurable goals and metrics in support of managing stakeholder expectations and satisfaction throughout the duration of the program.

- Identify key individual stakeholders and stakeholder groups.
- Understand stakeholder goals and expectations throughout the program. Confirm both the formal and informal goals, expectations and concerns.
- Identify what stakeholders expect to achieve from the business changes in personal and business terms.
- Provide a comprehensive understanding of what to achieve and each stakeholder's role in making that happen.

Establish a process to assess and monitor stakeholder expectations to ensure the program outcomes remain aligned throughout the program's duration.

Key Resources

- Change Lead

Support Resources

- Human Performance Architect
- Performance Measurement Lead

- Program Manager
- Quality Manager
- Resource Manager

Core Deliverables

Input
- Stakeholder Expectations Matrix
- Program Roadmap

Output
- Stakeholder Expectations Matrix
- Stakeholder List

Vital Steps

Identify Stakeholder Groups

A stakeholder group consists of people with a common purpose or goal and significant involvement or interest in the success of the program and projects. They are spokespersons representing a larger group. The group they represent must be comfortable with the selected representatives approving and signing off any program deliverables and decisions.

Do not limit the group to only the immediate people or functions with which you work. Include groups that are instigating (directly or indirectly) or affected by the change. Examples of stakeholder groups include the client IT organization, third party suppliers, outsourced units, asset owners, customers, etc.

Identify potential stakeholder groups by asking the following questions:

- Who participates in the work?
- Who receives or signs off on the work?
- Who uses the work when we finish?
- Who defends the work if something goes wrong?
- Who uses the work?
- Who upgrades and maintains the work?
- Whose career path is affected by the work?
- Who includes the work status within their management reporting?
- Who supplies inputs to this work?
- Whom is this work critically dependent upon?

Though not a complete list of responsibilities, stakeholders typically include groups or individuals who complete the following:

- Sponsor the project
- Generate, review, and approve requirements
- Participate in the decision making process
- Develop the application (e.g., project team members)
- Use the application
- Are affected by the application
- Support the application.

For each stakeholder group, identify the following:

- Individuals who can best articulate the key expectations. For each individual stakeholder, select the appropriate expectation gathering technique (interview, questionnaire, focus group, etc.) and identify any preliminary expectation(s) he or she may have.
- Identify individuals who can comfortably sign off that the program accurately captures the expectations of the stakeholder group. Include individuals who are listed as individual stakeholders.

Gather Program Expectations and Goals

The specific approach varies depending on existing relationships with senior management and the experience from prior change initiatives.

Activity 1 - Begin by analysing the Program Roadmap and (if available) the Stakeholder Expectations Matrix deliverable. The matrix outlines the program goals and expectations for the senior leaders, sponsors, and key buyers within the organization. The Contract may also provide some insight into senior executive goals and expectations.

Consider which members of senior management to involve in this initial work. Select people with the decision-making power to proceed. Understand (in their terms) the business problems they face, the business results they wish to achieve, and their expectations on the conduct or execution of the program. Uncover individual perceptions, expectations, and facts. Involve as many of the senior managers needed to determine the current level of consensus regarding the change. The most important objective is to determine what stakeholders want (in terms of both business results and personal agendas) and to ensure that their goals and expectations are consistent with what they say the organization should achieve.

Ask the senior management the following questions:

- What are the organization's corporate strategy, business unit strategy, and/or operating vision? Is it viable? What additional work, if any, is required before the process proceeds?
- How does this proposed change contribute to achieving the business strategy?
- What does senior management anticipate as the business goals and expectations of the change?
- What are senior management's expectations for program delivery and quality?
- What change areas contribute the most value to the organization?
- What leadership and governance expectations exist? Who is involved? How frequently are meetings held?
- What relationship aspects are most important?
- What sponsor requirements or expectations around work authorization, time frame review processes, discussion venues, exit criteria, sign-off procedures, and commit points exist?
- What personal expectations and perceptions exist regarding the change?
- How well do/does the senior executives and/or the project team understand the business goals (from the senior manager's point of view)?
- To what extent do senior executives and/or the program or project teams concur with senior management's interpretation of these program goals (from the senior manager's point of view)?
- How are decisions made throughout the program to effect change?

Activity 2 - Gather and document the expectations of key program executors to ensure execution remains in alignment with key sponsors. Depending on the level or position of the executors, use the relevant key questions from the key senior management questions listed above.

Activity 3: Gather and document the expectations of primary and secondary stakeholders. Depending on the groups involved, select individuals from each group to represent a particular area during facilitated meetings. Because you are also interested in getting their individual perceptions, one-on-one meetings may work better than facilitated group meetings. If there are several individuals or groups, select a representative cross-section to attend the facilitated group meetings.

Consider drafting a short survey and setting up meeting times and sessions where the specific groups will complete the survey. Questions to ask primary and secondary stakeholders include:

- What are the organization's corporate strategy, business unit strategy, and/or operating vision? Is it viable? What additional work, if any, is required before the process proceeds?
- What is their understanding of the program goals?
- How does this proposed program contribute to achieving the business strategy?
- What personal expectations and perceptions do they have regarding the program?
- Do they believe that the change will positively or negatively affect them? How?
- What are critical elements or activities to implement for the change's success?
- What is their perception regarding the sponsorship of the program? Is it strong? How can it be improved?

Activity 4: Agree/confirm the high-level formal expectations and verify the criteria that the individual stakeholders wish to be used to assess whether they are being met. Challenge and renegotiate any expectations that are deemed, by either party, to be unrealistic.

Activity 5: Review the applicable Program Roadmap, Business Case, client satisfaction improvement plan, and client plan documents to identify any significant expectations not already captured. For each expectation, determine the most appropriate stakeholder to validate your assumptions. Contact each stakeholder, and confirm your captured key delivery, relationship, and value expectations. With each contact, verify the criteria to use to assess whether the expectations are met. Challenge and renegotiate any unrealistic expectations.

Activity 6: Update/create the Stakeholder Expectations Matrix deliverable as needed.

Activity 7: Communicate the results to other workstreams and executives. Pay particular attention to teams working to develop the business case to ensure a clear understanding of the stakeholders' expectations.

Assign Responsibility for Stakeholder Management

Stakeholder Management identifies and manages the key stakeholders for the program so that the program operates in a supportive climate, does not face unexpected resistance, and has access to information, personnel, and other resources. To accomplish this, create a one-on-one relationship between a senior sponsor/change agent from the program and each key stakeholder.

Stakeholder Management is a two-way communication process. It is as important to listen to the key stakeholders and understand their issues as to inform them of the program/project's purpose and how it progresses. These steps reduce rework and ensure the program satisfies the organization's needs.

Establish a process to manage and track these expectations up front so that all parties have an understanding of the steps that will be taken as the program is underway. It is essential that the people from the program who are assigned to work with the key stakeholders are:

- Fully committed to the program themselves
- Knowledgeable about the program/project
- Trusted by their key stakeholders
- Credible when talking about the program

Consider the following activities to establish a stakeholder management process:

- Identify suitable Key Stakeholder Managers (KSMs) for each key stakeholder. KSMs have an established working relationship and/or expertise in a related field that creates a similarity of interest/perspective with the assigned key stakeholder.
- Educate the KSMs about change processes, the change commitment curve, and their role and responsibilities as KSMs. Identify the benefits to the program, the company, and themselves of succeeding in their roles as KSMs.
- Help the KSMs identify, as a team, which behaviours correspond to which levels of the change commitment curve (Awareness, Understanding, Buy-in, and Commitment) for this particular program/project. If the team chooses to create one, use the Stakeholder Profile as input. Determine the behaviours needed from the key stakeholders with regard to the program.
- Identify the level of knowledge and commitment the key stakeholders currently display based on observable behaviours. Help the KSMs plan how (i.e., methods and frequency of interaction and key messages/experiences) to move their key stakeholders from the key stakeholder current level of commitment to the targeted level of commitment by a particular target date. Set target dates to have key stakeholders at interim commitment levels.
- Update the Stakeholder Profile (if created) to include an at-a-glance picture of the targeted commitment levels for the whole group of stakeholders, including the dates for the interim target

levels. This enables the KSM team to manage the key stakeholders' commitment levels as a whole. Remember that failure with any one stakeholder could create a major problem for the program.
- Ensure that the KSMs are fully conversant with the program and its value to the organization. This understanding includes the reason for doing the program (the context, or why), what the program aims to achieve (content, or what), and the ways the work will be done (the course of action, the details of who, what, where, and when). In addition, know the program's key milestones and interdependencies.
- Set up a mechanism to track the KSMs contacts with the key stakeholders and obtain feedback about their issues and commitment level. Ensure the mechanism is accessible and as easy as possible for the KSMs to use.
- Update the Stakeholder Expectations Matrix deliverable with the appropriate information

Establish Process for Monitoring Stakeholder Expectations and Satisfaction

Stakeholder expectation management involves gathering and understanding expectations and monitoring stakeholder expectations and satisfaction. Managing expectations directly affects the overall satisfaction of stakeholders.

Monitor stakeholder expectations and ensure expectations remain realistic by analysing progress on expectations, monitoring stakeholder perceptions and satisfaction, keeping expectations up to date and relevant, implementing improvements to address expectations that are not at the desired level, and communicating expectation status

Include the following activities when defining a process for monitoring Stakeholder Expectation and Satisfaction:

- Identify the processes, prioritization, feedback (satisfaction) mechanism, measure of success, goal, and the individual responsible for monitoring each expectation.
- Define the program metrics and feedback mechanism, and create procedures to assess and measure the progress of the program toward meeting or exceeding stakeholder expectations and satisfaction. Seek to use metrics already defined by the client, the business case, the contract, and/or program performance reporting.

- Determine the frequency and timing of formal reviews of the expectations and progress toward meeting those expectations. Review once per quarter, at major program/project milestones, or when scope changes significantly.
- Several program management functions support the measurement of progress towards meeting expectations and the relationship of expectations to goals. Examples include: •Delivery Management
    - Value Management
    - Resource Management
    - Quality Management
    - Leadership and Governance

Confirm Goals and Expectations with Stakeholders

The process for confirming goals and expectations needs to be driven by the stakeholders. Some techniques to use include interviews, surveys, prioritization schemes, or a combination of methods.

Have stakeholders review and confirm the final list of expectations, goals, and the feedback approach. Stakeholders confirm that the program benefits and values will meet expectations.

Stakeholders should then confirm and validate the prioritized list of expectations and values. This prioritized list will be used to facility future discussions concerning trade-offs between cost, resources, value and benefits as the program progresses. Conduct individual and/or group discussions to resolve differences and reach consensus on the expectations.

Update the Stakeholder Expectations Matrix deliverable as needed.

Communicate Process, Goals, and Expectations

Use the Communications Plan as a guide to develop the communications materials and communicate the approved, agreed upon, and prioritized expectations to all stakeholders and program participants.

Update the Risk Log with any risks associated with meeting stakeholder goals and expectations.

Key Points to Consider

Develop a Stakeholder Profile.

In addition to the Stakeholder Expectations Matrix, consider creating a Stakeholder Profile based on the preliminary information that the team has about the various stakeholder groups. The document contains the following information:

- How change affects the stakeholders (High, Medium, Low)
- The stakeholder's role during the change process (Sponsor, Agent, Target)
- The stakeholder's current level of commitment (High, Medium, Low)
- The stakeholder's current versus the desired level of commitment or reaction to change

Have other workstreams (such as Quality, Delivery Management, Leadership and Governance, etc.) consider using or creating a similar document that contains information more relevant to the goals of that particular work group.

1. Based on the updated Stakeholder Expectations Matrix document, assess the degree of impact the change has on each stakeholder group. Provide clear definitions regarding Low, Medium, and High impact, and consider elements such as changes to processes, Key Performance Indicators, rewards, and/or incentives as inputs into the degree of impact.
2. Identify the role of the particular stakeholder group: Sponsor, Agent, Champion, or Target.
    a. Sponsors are respected leaders of the organization whose support legitimizes the change.
    b. Agents implement the change. Agents can only execute the change, not sponsor it.
    c. Champions exert extensive influence in the organization and advocate a change's acceptance by speaking positively about and supporting the change.
    d. Targets actually change. This group includes sponsors, agents, champions, individual employees, and customers of the processes.
3. Assess the current level of commitment each group has toward the change and the desired level of commitment for a successful program or project.
4. Assess or anticipate the current or typical reaction to change of a particular stakeholder group to changes that occur in the organization. Identify the desired reaction from that group.

The benefits of completing this profile include:

- Help in conducting the detailed Change Impact Assessment
- Help in driving the appropriate communication strategy
- Help in defining the change initiatives that need to be implemented in the early stages of the program to obtain stakeholder acceptance
- Serving as a tool to manage expectations on an ongoing basis

Vary the approach depending on senior management involvement.

If there has been very little involvement by the senior managers, focus on defining the program's goals and expectations from the senior managers instead of identifying and analysing primary and secondary stakeholder expectations.

Perform further discussion and activities when perceptions and expectations differ among members of the senior management group. Help them align their expectations and agree on changes to commit to.

Once there is a clear understanding of senior management or leadership goals, expectations, roles, and the overall decision-making process, the teams obtain information concerning primary and secondary stakeholder goals and expectations.

Because this task is shared across all workstreams, derive the stakeholders' detailed goals and expectations from similar activities conducted by other teams. Work together to capture this information to avoid work repetition.

Establish and manage stakeholder expectations.

- Stakeholder views will change during the course of the program. Update and review Stakeholder Expectations Matrix deliverable accordingly. If a Stakeholder Profile exists, also update and review that document.
- Stakeholders want to know how changes affect them. Ask stakeholders for their input whenever possible, as this helps stakeholders contribute personal input to the change process.
- Articulate to the top 10 individual stakeholders the legitimate personal wins resulting from the implemented changes.
- Conduct stakeholder meetings to clarify issues and fears, and to alleviate concerns. Move stakeholders to the point of imagining and mentally trying out the changes.

- Develop plans to leverage the positive attitudes of enthusiastic stakeholders.
- Provide the stakeholders with continuous invitations to become involved and reassurance that they will get their results.

Gather goals and expectations.

When defining the expectation management process, take into account (but do not limit considerations to) the following elements:

- Which stakeholder expectations will be collected?
- Who gathers the stakeholder expectations?
- How will expectations be categorized?
- How will expectations be prioritized?
- What is the protocol for evaluating progress on expectations?
- How are expectations shared with the program team and stakeholders?
- How are expectations tracked and monitored?
- Who oversees the expectation management process?
- What are the predefined intervals for revisiting expectations for relevance?
- How will expectations that are not being met be addressed?

Use the appropriate data gathering tools and techniques.

You can use many different tools and techniques to gather expectations and define the performance metrics. Choose a technique you are comfortable using that is appropriate for the personalities of the individuals concerned.

Capture and validate unstated expectations and values.

Unstated expectations are not expressly communicated. Many stakeholders have unstated expectations that are difficult to gather and analyse. Have team members look for unstated expectations and work with stakeholders to get these expectations articulated and documented.

Review the critical goals and expectations.

Any critical expectation that requires review and sign-off from the program governance team has at least one measure to credibly provide feedback on its overall progress. For each metric, determine the performance levels that the stakeholder would rate as very dissatisfied, dissatisfied, neutral, satisfied, and very satisfied. Identify any relevant performance review points that require review with the program governance team.

Assess Current Leadership Capabilities

Aims and Objectives

Define the program-critical leadership skills and success factors.

Identify and document gaps between the current and future leadership capabilities.

Key Resources

- Change Lead

Inputs

- Stakeholder Expectations Matrix
- Program Roadmap
- Business Case
- Contract

Outputs

- Capability Assessment Approach
- Current Capability Assessment

Vital Steps

Identify Critical Skills and Success Factors

Program and project leaders need the right skills to make the overall program successful. The sponsoring organization may not have the leadership capability needed to accomplish the program successfully. This step identifies the critical skills necessary to lead a program successfully.

The leadership and management skills required differ based on the context of the program.

Programs require leadership and management skills. To identify the critical leadership and management skills and success factors, the team needs to understand the business and organizational context in which the program operates. Skill requirements differ by leader role, so skill sets may include the following:

- Governance Team---Value management, demand management, financial management, change journey management, communication
- Program Management Team---Stakeholder management, quality management, resource management, financial management, risk

management, inter-culture management, change journey management, communication
- Project Management Team---Organizational, inter-culture management, interpersonal skills, communication, problem solving, coaching, negotiation, virtual teaming

Validate with Senior Leadership

Senior leadership must agree on the critical leadership capabilities and be willing to invest in leadership development initiatives. Leadership development initiatives can only be successful if the senior leadership commits to implementing them. Lack of support produces little or no results.

Senior leadership may already have ideas about the critical skills necessary to run the program and gaps that exist. Sometimes they will not be as aware of the intricacies of leading a large program. This step creates a common understanding of the critical skills needed for the specific program with senior leadership. Provide senior leadership with best practices and lessons learned from previous experiences to increase their understanding of the complexity involved in leading a large program.

Senior leadership ensures that the identified leadership skills link to the program's long-term strategic objectives. It is likely that people who sit on governance, program, or project management teams will have operational roles once the program completes. Therefore, the leadership skills need to be mastered by the time the program is over.

Define Leadership Capability Assessment Approach

Determine an appropriate approach to assess the current leadership capabilities. The decision regarding which assessment approach to use is influenced by the scale and potential impact of the program and by the perception of the senior leadership regarding current leadership capabilities.

The approach ranges from interviewing senior leadership to performing an in-depth assessment of current skills. Target those individuals with governance, program, or project management responsibility who influence the overall program's success. Consider the percentage of time that resources are committed to the program.

Where possible, leverage existing client performance management and professional development frameworks, tools, and processes, rather than creating a customized approach.

Conduct Leadership Capability Assessments

Depending on the approach selected and number of leaders targeted, assessment can take a few days or a few weeks. The more in-depth and analytical the assessment, the longer it takes to complete.

Be sensitive to how you conduct the assessments. Some may feel threatened by the assessment, so address that this is not an individual performance evaluation. Educate the target audience on the vision and mission of the program and how critical their roles and skills are in achieving the strategic objectives of the program. Obtaining their buy-in on the program's strategic objectives helps gain their support throughout the assessment period.

Review Gaps

Assess the findings from the leadership capability assessments to identify where gaps exist. Although the sponsoring organization may already have insights on individual results, concern yourself with the overall results. If you have information on the leadership role that each person will perform (governance, program, project), tally the results based on these groupings to make it easier to interpret the results and define leadership development needs for each group.

Define Governance Approach

Aims and Objectives

Define the vision that acts as the foundation for designing the governance team.
Identify the stakeholder groups represented in the governance team.
Define the governance team structure, and identify appropriate members.

Key Resources

- Change Lead

Support Resources

- Business Architect
- Change Specialist
- Human Performance Architect

Inputs

- Stakeholder Expectations Matrix
- Program Roadmap
- Business Case
- Contract

Outputs

- Governance Approach

Vital Steps

Review Key Stakeholder Expectations

Review the Stakeholder Expectations Matrix to ensure that the key stakeholder expectations for the program are understood. These expectations shape how the governance team, program, and project leaders direct the program and projects. Stakeholder expectations define program success from each key stakeholder group's perspective.

Define Team Vision

Use the Team Vision or Mission Statement as a guiding principle to assist the governance team and leadership with achieving their goals and expectations for the program and project(s).

Define Guiding Coalition

Identify the stakeholder groups to represent in the governance organization. Include leaders and decision makers from the sponsoring organization. The governance group's membership results in a cross-functional team with a corporate view. To do this step:

- List all key stakeholder groups to include in the governance organization.
- Assess the business reason why each stakeholder group is part of the governance organization. As you assess who to include in the guiding coalition, consider program funding sources, the groups most impacted by the program and degree of change to their respective business processes/systems, parties with special skills or decision making/approval roles (Risk, Quality, etc.), and organizational politics.
- Identify the risks and benefits associated with including these groups in the governance organization.
- Present the final list of stakeholder groups to senior leadership for approval.

Define Team Structure and Roles

Defining governance team structure and roles is influenced by the context of the sponsoring organization and by the program's strategic objectives. When defining the structure and roles, consider the following:

- Governance Team Lead Role. Identify a leader within the governance team. This person keeps the governance team focused and working directly with program sponsor(s). Depending on the program, a co-leadership model may be used (e.g., an IT and Business Leader working together).
- Facilitator Role. Consider using a Facilitator (part of the team or pulled from PMO or Program/Project teams) to support the governance team. The Facilitator supports the Governance Team Lead and keeps the governance team focused, facilitates team meetings and decision making, and documents agreed actions. The Facilitator may use a Scribe (which can be a rotational role) or serve in this capacity as well.
- Sponsor. Establish one sponsor for each project. This person has an objective perspective, owns the strategic vision/plan, enforces adherence to the vision/principles, comes from the business and is credible, visible, and has a sustained role in the project/program.

- Governance Membership. Ensure it represents critical stakeholders, and that members are actively engaged and accountable. Membership is of manageable size, and the cross-functional project team has a broad corporate view.
- Business Architects. These people act as single points of contact for the businesses across technologies and understand and represent the businesses.

Determine whether one or more governance team levels are needed. Large programs may need more than one level of advisory committees set up around projects. If two levels of committees are established, the lead on the lower level committee(s) participates as a member of the more senior governance team, to ensure continued alignment.

In addition, define the relationship between the program governance team (and other sub-committees) and other programs that may be working within the organization. In some cases, overlapping membership at the governance level ensures alignment across the programs, particularly when there is significant overlapping of stakeholder groups.

Identify Team Members

List all the potential candidates for governance team membership and discuss how each would contribute to the governance organization. Consider the skills and perspective that each individual brings to bear for the program. This exercise produces the final list of candidates to propose to senior leadership as members of the governance organization. When finalizing candidates, note that:

- Project sponsor and leaders who set aggressive standards are necessary up and down the governance organization.
- The mix results in an effective cross-functional executive team that is driven by the broader business goals and that facilitates tight co-ordination between technology, operations, and the business areas.
- Members at all levels must understand how business strategy links to systems and operations.

Define Decision Making Authority

This step determines who makes what decisions and the process for making these decisions. Determine decision making authority based on the area of responsibility. Document the decision making authority and decision making process, and communicate it thoroughly so people can follow the process. Confusion about decision making authority can result in an unnecessary lead time for decisions to be made.

Validate Structure and Members with Senior Leadership

Obtain senior leadership sign-off on the structure and membership of the governance organization as well as the expected deliverables to be utilized by this structure to manage the strategic direction of the program and its projects.

Develop Leadership Initiatives

Aims and Objectives

Ensure leadership development objectives and initiatives link directly to the capabilities needed to achieve the program objectives.
Review leadership best practices, explore leadership development solution options, and determine the most appropriate leadership development initiatives for the organization.
Identify leadership learning and development assets needed for the initiatives.
Create role-based leadership development plans.
Develop or source leadership development assets.
Define an approach to evaluate the effectiveness of the leadership development initiatives.

Resources
- Change Lead

Supporting roles
- Change Specialist
- Human Performance Architect

Inputs
- Stakeholder Expectations Matrix
- Governance Approach
- Change Acceptance Strategy
- Current Capability Assessment
- Business Case
- Contract
- Program Communications Plan
- Program Roadmap
- Change Plan

Outputs
- Leadership Development Initiatives
- Leadership Development Plans
- Leadership Development Materials

Confirm Leadership Development Objectives

This step ensures that leadership development objectives align with the overall vision and mission of the program. To complete this step, do the following:

- Define leadership development objectives, both overall and by role, and confirm with senior leadership that they align with the strategic vision for the program.
- Assess potential barriers to the achievement of these objectives, given organizational culture, leadership style, and change history.
- Assess the impact of these objectives on the current performance management process, and recommend changes to performance management, if necessary.
- Refine the leadership development objectives to make them realistic and measurable.

Review Leadership Development Options

Review best practices and lessons learned from past experiences to identify options for leadership development. Gain an understanding of the client's existing programs to comprehend the potential for closing gaps later---particularly for organizations that invest in and focus on leadership development. The level of investment for your program may vary depending on client's perception of:

- The gaps between current and required leadership capability
- How critical these leadership capability gaps are to the program's success
- The relative importance of leadership development initiatives against other initiatives that the program undertakes
- The perception of the overall organization's capabilities, reputation, and culture

Present leadership development options together with costs, benefits, level of effort and duration, risks, etc., so that the senior leadership sponsor can analyse the options. Where possible, leverage existing options within the client organization for training, coaching, etc.

Define Leadership Development Initiatives

The selection of the leadership development initiatives is driven by the program complexity, investment level, organizational culture, and the availability of the appropriate resources. Leadership development initiatives can range from self-development to one-to-one coaching to leadership development workshops.

A sponsor who is strongly committed to the leadership development initiative may create personal development plans based on the gaps assessed at the individual level and may implement a process to monitor their progress. A sponsor may also decide to address leadership development at the team or group level, as opposed to the individual level.

Consider the complexity of the program in selecting the right leadership development initiatives. If the program involves offshore delivery centres, leaders need to understand the business ethics and working style of teams from different cultures and have the appropriate interpersonal skills to lead global teams effectively.

Leadership roles dictate the critical skills needed. For example, visioning skills are more critical to people who sit on the governance team than project managers who manage the day-to-day work of their project teams.

Assign ownership to each initiative. If there are multiple owners of the leadership development initiatives, document who owns which piece, and make sure owners know their roles and responsibilities in implementing the initiatives. If there are timing dependencies between initiatives, make sure everyone understands what these dependencies are. Obtain senior leadership approval on the ownership of each initiative.

While both leadership and management skills are important for leading a change program, understand the difference between the two:

- Leaders
    - Create and communicate a vision
    - Establish a sense of urgency
    - Take risks
    - Seek opportunities
    - Change organizational rules
    - Provide something to believe in
    - Inspire achievement
- Managers
    - Control risk
    - React to opportunities
    - Enforce organizational rules
    - Coordinate efforts
    - Seek and then follow directions

Identify Learning/Development Assets Needed

Determine the learning/development assets required for the initiatives. The budget allocated for leadership development initiative also influences the selection of the assets.

- List the required assets and document the objective of each asset. Assets may include training, reading materials, tools (e.g., for

collaboration or knowledge sharing), surveys (e.g., 360 degree assessments, leadership styles surveys, personality tests), coaching programs, etc.
- Investigate if the assets are already available within the organization.
- Estimate the cost and time to obtain or develop them.
- List potential vendors for the assets.
- List any potential issues and risks related to the assets.
- Chart a timeline when these assets are available.

Create Role-based Leadership Development Plans

Create a Leadership Development Plan for each role. Obtain senior leadership approval of these plans. The leadership development program participants can use these plans as the basis for their development plans. The Leadership Development Plan includes a list of leadership and management courses, reading materials, and time frame associated with the plan.

Decide whether to create a Personal Development Plan. This is a custom plan for each individual based on the leadership assessment conducted during gap analysis. The Personal Development Plan includes a list of recommended development priorities (e.g., personal actions for development, training programs, reading, and timescale).

The internal performance management process typically handles the monitoring of personal development plans. The project may be responsible for facilitating the process, but not for monitoring the progress at the individual level.

Source Leadership Development Assets

This step ensures the defined assets are available in a timely manner. If they already exist within the organization (and just never were deployed), review and revise as appropriate. If they are not available, obtain the right resources to produce them. The program team works closely with the team members or vendors who develop the assets to ensure they meet the intended objectives.

Thoroughly review the assets, and have them approved by the senior leadership. Pilot the assets to select individuals before the actual roll-out. If assets are culturally sensitive, have a diverse target audience in the pilot group.

Define Leadership Initiatives Evaluation Approach

Define an approach to evaluate each of the initiatives to ensure they meet the stated objectives. The program decides what to stop, change, or continue based on the feedback received. Evaluations ensure that leadership initiatives meet their objectives.

Key Points to Consider

Communicate leadership initiatives.

Prepare communications about leadership initiatives. Work with the communication team on key messages and timing so that everyone knows what the initiatives are about and is ready to participate.

Incorporate initiatives around intercultural leadership, when needed.

When involving offshore delivery centres in the program, incorporate initiatives around intercultural leadership. Programs involving offshore delivery centres can fail because of the lack of understanding on how to lead in multi-cultural environments. Prepare for this challenge, if needed.

Implement the Governance Organization

Aims and Objectives

Establish a charter to guide the operation of the governance team.

Launch the governance team by communicating the team charter to the program and project members and stakeholders.

Monitor and resolve any issues that arise during implementation, and refine the team charter accordingly.

Resources

- Change Lead

Supporting resources

- Business Owner
- Change Specialist
- Client Director
- Program Manager
- Project Manager

Inputs

- Governance Approach
- Leadership Development Initiatives
- Stakeholder Expectations Matrix
- Business Case
- Contract
- Program Roadmap

Outputs

- Governance Charter
- Sign-off Sheet

<u>Vital Steps</u>

Conduct Governance Kick-off Meeting

Invite the people appointed to serve as the members of the governance organization to participate in the governance kick-off meeting. Communicate the meeting agenda and any expected preparation. At this time, these people are aware that the governance organization being established will play a critical role in leading the program and driving the business case. The kick-off meeting helps the members to understand the objectives of the program, agree on how this team operates, and commit their participation in the governance organization.

Leadership initiatives can launch at the same time as the kick-off meeting. Incorporate these initiatives in the agenda, and allocate time accordingly. Take note of the potential disruptions when scheduling the meeting since a significant number of leadership members are involved.

Ideally, conduct the meeting off-site. Taking people away from the day-to-day workplace increases focus on the task at hand.

Prepare the materials carefully. While the governance team needs to understand the details of the program (e.g., as outlined in the business case), presenting details can be daunting. Present this information in a summary format and have details ready as a back-up when needed.

Facilitate and effectively lead the meeting to keep the team focused on reaching agreement on the governance charter and committed to their respective roles in this governance organization.

Create Governance Charter(s)

Having all governance organization members shape the charter helps increase their sense of ownership of the charter itself. Ensure everyone understands the strategic objectives of the program and the vision and mission of the governance organization before detailing out the team's charter. The charter may contain the following:

- Governance Business Objectives
- Decision Making Processes
- Team roles and membership
- Operating Guiding Principles
- Key Activities
- Key Deliverables
- Milestones and Team Calendar
- Metrics for program success and governance team success
- Risk and issue management processes

Obtain Senior Leadership Approval

The charter undergoes several iterations before it is considered final. Senior leadership or the program sponsor validates and approves the draft charter before initiating communications. Use a cascading communication approach to provide opportunity for dialog and capture feedback from the working teams.

Communicate Governance Charter(s)

Once the charter is finalized, approved, and ready to be implemented, communicate the charter to the program and project stakeholders.

Monitor Implementation and Resolve Issues

The leader and the facilitator for the governance team monitor the team progress and work to address any issues that emerge. Depending on the issue, this may involve one-on-one discussions, coaching, or refining the charter.

It may take awhile for the governance members to understand their roles and the decision- making process. Even if they understand their roles, it takes time to become used to the process.

Assign short-term tasks to governance members so that they can practice their roles and increase their understanding of the process. Communicating the governance team's charter is the first opportunity for team members to act as leaders and demonstrate ownership.

If issues arise during implementation, detect whether the issue is due to:

- Learning curve of the new roles and responsibilities
- Lack of clarity in the decision making process and authority
- Lack of ownership and commitment
- Lack of communication

Upon understanding the root cause of the issue, implement actions to resolve the issue. Work with the stakeholder acceptance and management team if the issues are around ownership and commitment.

Key Points to consider

Implement governance organization in a timely manner.

Plan for the amount of time needed to complete this task. The initial set-up and implementation of a new governance enables the rest of the downstream team to effectively hit their targeted goals.

A delay in the completion of this task can affect the overall time frame for the program.

Continuously improve the governance structure and processes.

Survey governance members during early implementation to assess what worked and what did not, as well as to gather suggestions for improvement. At the end of the initial roll-out, the program has insights into what needs to be done to make the governance structure more effective. Clearly document and communicate changes to the governance structure, process, standards, and policies based on findings from the early implementation.

Work with the stakeholder acceptance team to accelerate take-up of governance roles.

The leadership development initiatives increase readiness and prepare the governance team members for performing their new leadership roles. As individuals respond to change differently, some members may be more ready than others in accepting their new roles. Work with the stakeholder acceptance team to assess the commitment level of the governance members. Consider incorporating the change initiatives during the roll-out process.

Use the cascading communication approach to communicate the governance charter.

The cascading communication effectively communicates change. Not only do individuals listen better when obtaining communications from their direct supervisors, but the approach provides opportunity for dialog and the ability to capture feedback.

Implement Leadership Initiatives

Aims and Objectives

Roll out leadership development initiatives to the target audiences.

Evaluate leadership development initiatives to ensure they meet their objectives.

Ensure that performance management reinforces the desired leadership behaviours so the new behaviours are sustainable.

Resources

- Change Lead

Inputs

- Leadership Development Initiatives
- Leadership Development Plans
- Leadership Development Materials
- Leadership Initiatives Checklist

Outputs

- Leadership Development Initiatives
- Leadership Development Plans
- Leadership Development Materials

Vital Steps

Launch Leadership Initiatives

- Communicate the leadership development initiatives, and ensure the target audience is ready for the launch.
- Approve and make the Leadership Development Materials available for the launch.
- Prepare the instructors, coaches, and other resources (e.g., Human Resources) needed to support the launch.
- Complete testing for the tools and other technology-based assets prior to the launch.
- Confirm the schedules and participants for the events.
- Conduct the Leadership Initiatives launch events.

Evaluate Leadership Initiatives

Collect feedback from the participants and senior leadership, formally and informally. Evaluate which initiatives to stop, change, or continue as is. Document the lessons learned to use as input in the next steps.

Refine Leadership Initiatives

Revise the Leadership Development Plans based on the decisions made during the evaluation. Refine the materials accordingly.

If the leadership initiatives continue after the program completes, transition the materials to the operations team. Make sure they receive all the documentation necessary to run the initiatives after the program completes.

Align Performance Management with Desired Leadership Behaviours

To ensure the investment made for leadership development yields results, align performance management processes to reinforce the new behaviors. Use professional development plans, annual goal setting, and other performance management processes to reinforce expectations and make the initiatives real for the participants.

Work with the individuals responsible for performance management to ensure the desired leadership behaviours are properly evaluated during performance reviews and rewarded accordingly. This may include client HR contacts, the individual member's supervisors, etc.

Sustain Leadership Commitment

Sustain the desired leadership behaviours by properly reviewing and rewarding these behaviours.

Continuously monitor how effectively the governance team and the overall program and project leadership operate.

Identify and implement actions to improve the leadership capability and the effectiveness of the governance team.

Resource

- Change Lead

Inputs

- Governance Charter
- Program Roadmap
- Change Acceptance Strategy
- Business Case
- Contract
- Leadership Development Plans

Outputs

- Governance Charter
- Leadership Development Plans
- Leadership and Governance Scorecard

Vital Steps

Direct Program and Projects

This step reflects the governance team's day-to-day responsibilities for providing direction and sponsorship to the program, and to the program and project leaders.

Operate Governance

Governance serves as an advisory body and provides direction for the program. Governance members meet, resolve issues, and make decisions for the program. The governance team continuously monitors the program progress against the business case, and program plan, reviews the viability of proposed work, and makes go or no-go decisions.

Review and Reward Performance

Review performance and reward leaders for adopting the desired leadership behaviours. Work closely with the individuals responsible for performance management processes to ensure that the new behaviours are incorporated into the performance management process.

Evaluate Leadership and Governance Effectiveness

Continuously monitor how effectively the leadership and governance team operates, and make changes as necessary. Use metrics to evaluate the effectiveness of the leadership and governance. Recommend improvements for any measure that falls below the minimum standard.

Conduct evaluations with the leadership and governance stakeholders. Have everyone agree on the issues and create improvement plans together.

Refine Leadership and Governance

Review the governance charter to see if updates are needed. Document and communicate any changes to the governance structure, process, standards, and policies as a result of the early implementation. Obtain senior leadership approval on the final version of the charter.

Chapter 2
Demand Management

Develop Program and Project Inventory

Aims and Objective

Validate or create the Program Roadmap.

Identify all project requests and requirements by business area.

Define and approve objective and quantifiable evaluation criteria that is used to prioritize and rank projects

Resources

- Programme Manager

Supporting roles

- Deployment Lead
- Project Manager
- Release Manager

Inputs

- Stakeholder Expectations Matrix
- Business Case
- Requirements
- Contract
- Program Roadmap

Outputs

- Project List
- Project Evaluation Criteria
- Program Roadmap

This task assumes that PMO has been established, and there are existing program and projects.

Use this task to determine projects for an annual IT budget and for projects or requirements within a given program of work. The same principles apply to executing the steps, but the breadth and depth of execution depend on the scope---enterprise-level or program-level.

Vital Steps

Validate Program Roadmap

Review the current program roadmap to determine the business and technology imperatives and goals, the expected value and benefits to deliver, and the delivery time frame targets.

The roadmap ties the business' strategic vision with the technology capabilities required to achieve immediate and long-term goals to achieve that vision.

If a roadmap is not available, derive the information from existing business and technology strategy documents to define where to solicit project lists and how to evaluate projects.

Solicit Project Requests

Identify the requirements and project requests by business area. Gather these from key stakeholders, department heads, or unit leads. This includes all requests for system maintenance, enhancements, or new projects.

If a legal contract determines the program of work, the contract's defined work scope is critical in this step.

Determine the appropriate mechanism to solicit Project Requests and requirements. Collect requests and requirements in a consistent fashion from all parties. Collect a complete list of high-level names, detailed descriptions, categorizations, and business reasons/justifications.

Accumulate all project and initiative requests into a single, consolidated project inventory (the preliminary Project List).

Define Project Evaluation Criteria

Develop or refine the Project Evaluation Criteria based on the business context surrounding the program. Use these criteria to score/rank projects (initiatives) based on what they contribute to the stated program objectives. Prioritize the criteria to allow for objective scoring in later steps.

These criteria typically relate to financial benefits (such as Net Present Value and Return On Investment), the business strategy, the target technology architecture, the roadmap alignment, competitive advantage, and the payback period.

If the client or program has guiding principles, use these to determine the evaluation criteria.

Consider using a measure of importance for each criterion to prepare a weighted average score.

Approve Evaluation Criteria

The program's governance team and/or stakeholders need to approve the project evaluation criteria. Obtain buy-in from business unit leads and initiative requestors.

Distribute List for Review

The preliminary Project List is one of the two deliverables distributed at the end of this task. This is a consolidated list of all projects (and/or requirements) as requested. Send the preliminary Project List to all stakeholders and the affected project managers.

Distribute Evaluation Criteria

The Evaluation Criteria is the second deliverable at the end of this task. The Evaluation Criteria reinforce the process by which priorities are determined. Ensure that the program governance team and/or key stakeholders receive the final version of Project Evaluation Criteria.

Key Points to Consider

Stay within the scope of the program.

This task establishes a consolidated inventory of work for the current program. Though the program has a stated overall objective, business heads may incorporate tangential requirements that could delay prioritization efforts. If these requirements are truly tangential, their project scores should reflect a lower priority.

Be aware of enhancements that may be loaded into each project. Because standalone enhancements typically score low against the evaluation criteria, business stakeholders may try to load them into larger projects.

Include all requested work in the project list.

Terminology and the categorization of work differ from client to client. When creating an initial project list, if system maintenance is supported by the same set of resources (as are projects), include this work in the project list. Maintenance is sometimes called business as usual (BAU) or fix on fail.

Likewise, if enhancements are expected from these resources, include enhancement requests as part of the project list. Enhancements are usually lower work effort items, but cut-off points for documentation and project life cycle adherence differ by client.

Estimate each of these non-project requests individually or dedicate a subset of resources to these efforts. List each type as a single line item in the Project List, and prioritize each accordingly.

Prioritize Project List

Aims and Objectives

Score projects based on objective, quantifiable evaluation criteria.
Rank projects in order of weighted scores.
Distribute approved list to the key program stakeholders.

Resources
- Programme Manager

Supporting Roles

- Business Owner
- Change Lead
- Client Director
- Project Manager
- Release Manager

Inputs

- Project List
- Project Evaluation Criteria
- Business Case
- Budget

Outputs

- Project List
- Sign-off Sheet
- Decision Analysis and Resolution Report

Vital Steps

Score Projects Based on Evaluation Criteria
Use the evaluation criteria to assess each project. Create a composite score using a weighted average of scores for each criterion.

Prioritize the Project List
Rank the project requests by their weighted scores. Distribute the Project List for review by the Program governance team and/or key stakeholders. When prioritizing project candidates, use Decision Analysis and Resolution (DAR) technique. Decision Analysis and Resolution (DAR) is a structured and formalized process that helps organize decision-making when complicated issues with a variety of possible answers exist. Document the

process and findings and produce a Decision Analysis and Resolution Report.

Approve and Distribute Project List
The program governance team and/or key stakeholders review and approve the ranked projects. Distribute this approved list to key stakeholders and all contributors.

Plan Capacity and Utilization

Aim and Objectives

Identify demand (the project list) and supply (resources available to work on projects) for the program.
Align supply to the demand, considering technical, schedule, and resource constraints.
Develop a capacity plan.

Resource
- Programme Manager

Supporting resources
- Release Manager
- Resource Manager

Inputs
- Project List
- Budget

Outputs
- Resource Capacity Plan

Vital Steps

This task runs concurrently with the Align Budget task. In these two tasks, apply the capacity and budget constraints to the prioritized project list created earlier. This task focuses on the capacity component. It applies constraints to the program's requests and accounts for program and project interdependencies, resource schedules, and technical limitations to determine what to deliver.

Align Technical Capacity to Project List
Evaluate the technical dependencies to deliver projects as prioritized in the program Project List. Delivery constraints may include the following:
- Number of available testing environments
- Number and size of constraint modules
- Number of regions/environments for the migration path to production
- The technology difficulty

In some cases, deliver multiple projects at one time to accommodate a technical constraint and complete more work in the allotted time.

Align Schedule Capacity to Project List
Evaluate any schedule dependencies for each project and the program. Also, check for dependencies between other programs. Planned code freezes or area/office shutdowns may affect project delivery.

Align Resource Capacity to Project List
Evaluate resource dependencies for each project and the program. Consider the skills needed for each project. Use the organization chart to determine resource and skill capacity. Decide if and when the programs and projects need Subject Matter Experts (SMEs).

Develop Capacity Plan
Use the outputs from the three previous steps to create the capacity plan.

Distribute Capacity Plan
Distribute the capacity plan to the program governance team and/or key stakeholders for review.

Align Budget

Aim and objective

Update the original budget to reflect the capacity constraints and project requests.
Gain governance team and/or stakeholder approval for any budget changes

This task runs concurrently with the Planning Capacity and Utilization tasks. In these two tasks, apply the capacity and budget constraints to the prioritized project list created earlier. This task focuses on the budget component. Possible outcomes include the following:
• Update (increase) the original budget to do all (or more of) the requested project/program work.
• Remove the lower priority items from the current program to stay within the original budget.
• Update (reduce) the original budget because the cost to perform all prioritized projects is less than the original program budget.

Resources
- Programme Manager

Supporting resources
- Program Finance Lead
- Project Manager

Input
- Resource Capacity Plan
- Initial Estimate
- Project List
- Detailed Estimate

Output
- Budget

Vital Steps

Align Budget to Capacity Plan
Verify whether the current budget supports full capacity.
Determine how much extra capacity would result if the budget is increased.

Align Budget with Project List
Verify whether the current budget supports all project requests.

Determine the cut-off point in the project list where the current budget stops supporting the work. Base the cut-off point (if necessary) on what the budget allows. Determine what additional projects might increase the budget.

Create Budget
Create additional scenarios to the original budget to present to the program governance team and/or key stakeholders. Determine the following:
- If it is possible to complete additional projects if some higher priority projects trimmed scope
- Whether adding projects or trimming the scope is prudent

If additional budget is available from other projects

Approve and Distribute Budget
Acquire the program governance team and/or key stakeholder approval for the budget. Distribute the budget to all key stakeholders.

Finalize Project List

Aims and Objectives

Incorporate feedback based on the distributed project, budget, and capacity plan.
Obtain stakeholder review and approval of major decisions regarding delivery capacity.
Distribute the finalized list of projects, the budget, and the capacity plan.

Resources
- Programme Manager

Supporting resources
- Business Owner
- Change Lead
- Client Director
- Project Manager
- Release Manager
- Sponsor

Inputs
- Contract
- Project List
- Resource Capacity Plan
- Budget
- Project Evaluation Criteria

Outputs
- Contract
- Project List
- Resource Capacity Plan
- Budget

Vital Steps

Validate the Project List
Validate the project list based on the sponsoring organization's business priorities. Involve all the key stakeholders influencing the project list in the validation process. Clarify any conflicting priorities to ensure that all the key stakeholders are in agreement of what is contained in the project list.

Revise Budget
Revise the program budget to incorporate feedback from the program governance team and/or key stakeholders.

Revise Capacity Plan
Revise the capacity plan based on changes to the budget or project list.

Distribute Project List, Budget, and Capacity Plan
Distribute the revised deliverables to the program governance team and/or key stakeholders.

Printed in Great Britain
by Amazon